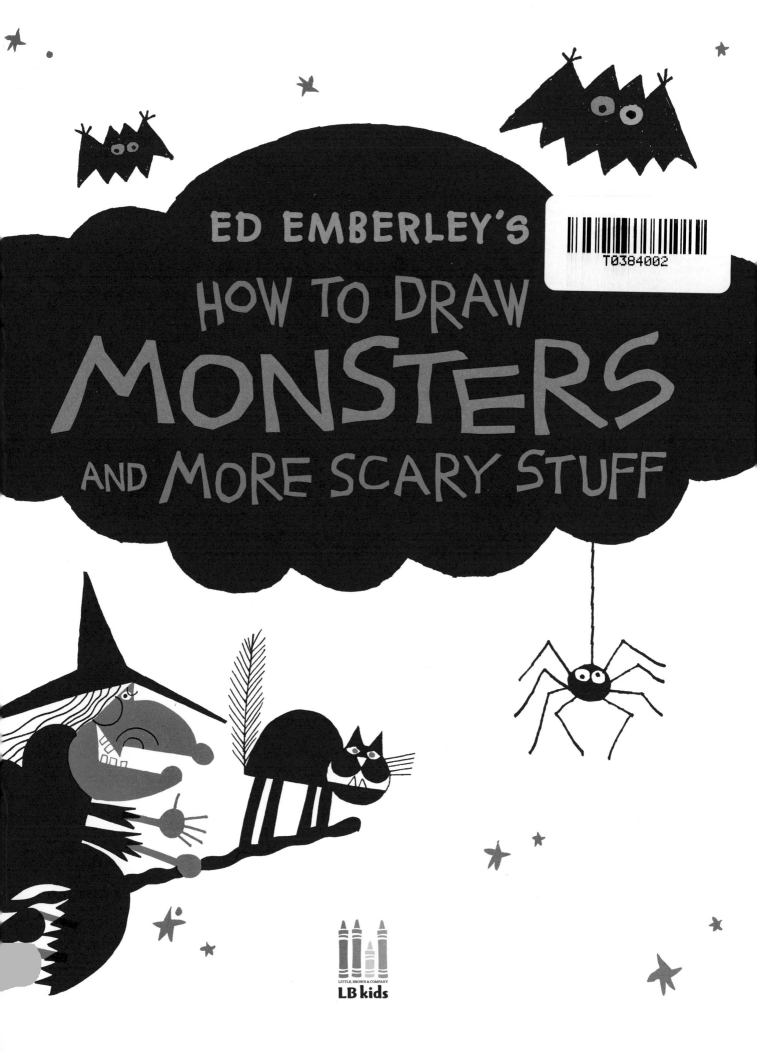

ED EMBERLEY'S
HOW TO DRAW
MONSTERS
AND MORE SCARY STUFF

T0384002

LITTLE, BROWN & COMPANY

LB kids

Little, Brown and Company
Hachette Book Group
1290 Avenue of the Americas, New York, NY 10104
Visit us at LBYR.com

Ed Emberley's Drawing Book of Halloween originally published in 1980 by Little, Brown and Company
Ed Emberley's Drawing Book of Weirdos originally published in 2002 by Little, Brown and Company
First Edition: July 2018

LB kids is an imprint of Little, Brown and Company.
The LB kids name and logo are trademarks of Hachette Book Group, Inc.

The publisher is not responsible for websites (or their content) that are not owned by the publisher.

Library of Congress Control Number: 2017961951

ISBN: 978-0-316-44344-9 (pbk.)

Printed in Dongguan, China

APS

10 9 8 7

IF YOU CAN DRAW THESE THINGS → △ ∧ S ⌣
YOU WILL BE ABLE TO DRAW   □ ⊓ . | ᴡᴡᴡ
ALL THE THINGS IN THIS BOOK.   O C D L

FOR INSTANCE —

↗ THE BOTTOM ROW TELLS WHAT TO DRAW

THE TOP ROW TELLS WHERE TO PUT IT.

VAMPIRE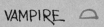

V V V V

▲▲

■

❚❚

▼▼▼ ▼▼▼▼

VAMPIRE

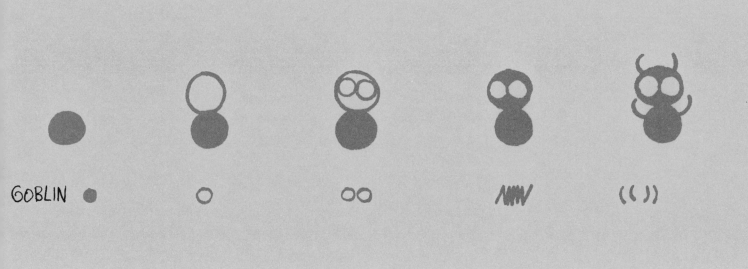

GOBLIN

CAT

MONSTER

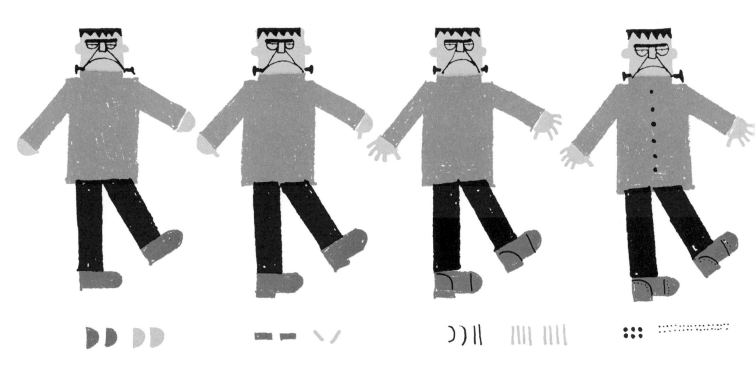

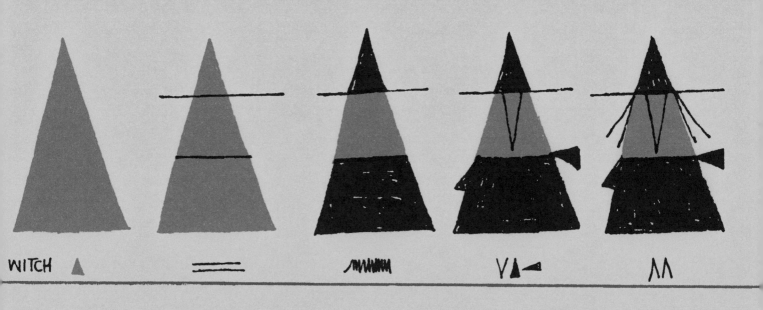

WITCH

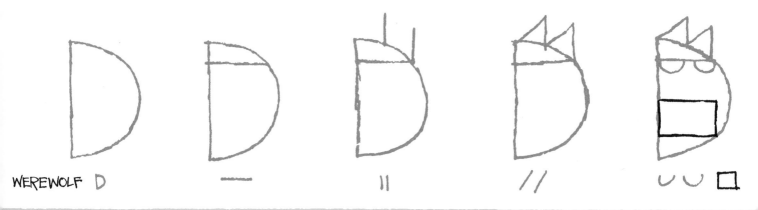

WEREWOLF

DEVIL

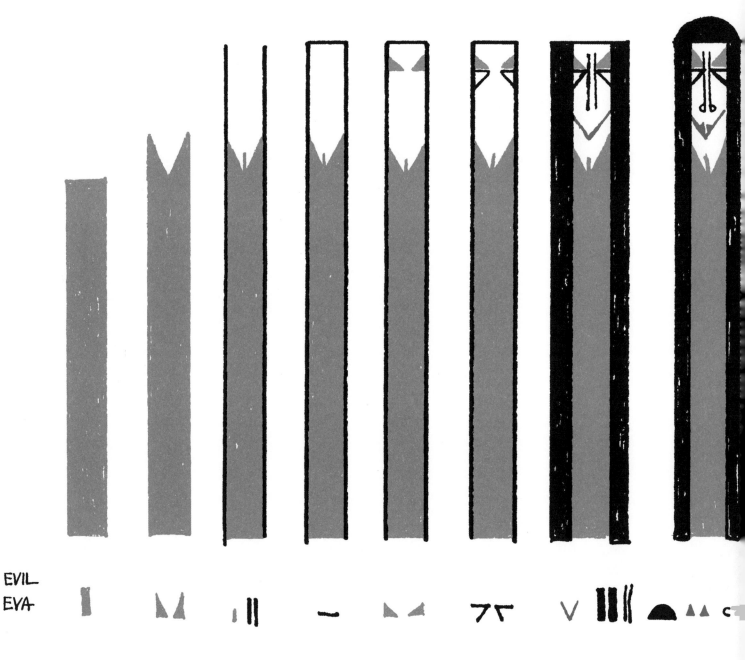

EVIL
EVA

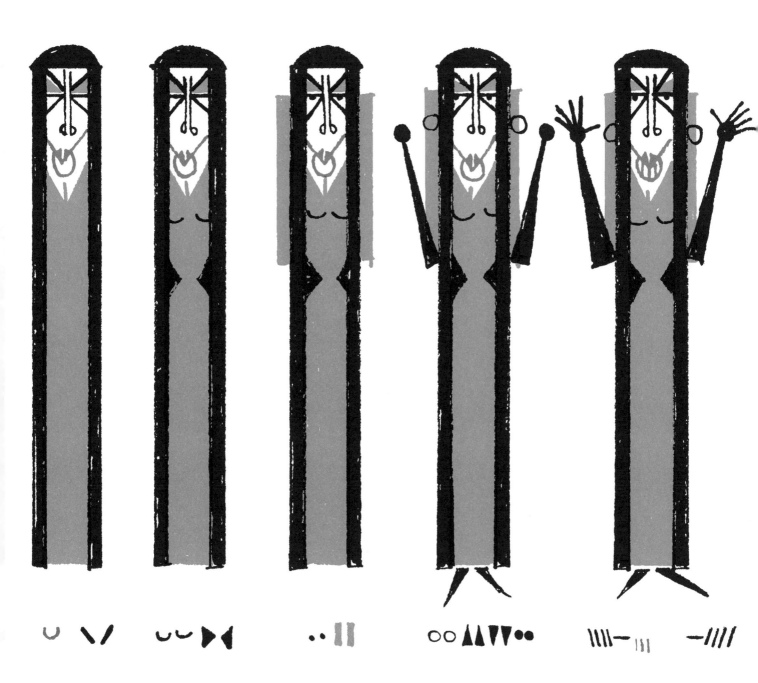

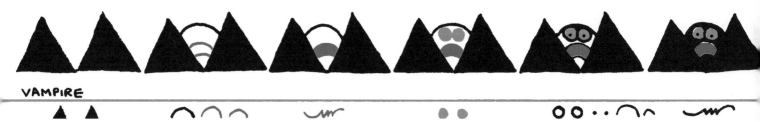

VAMPIRE

THE ZILLA

KING CONGO

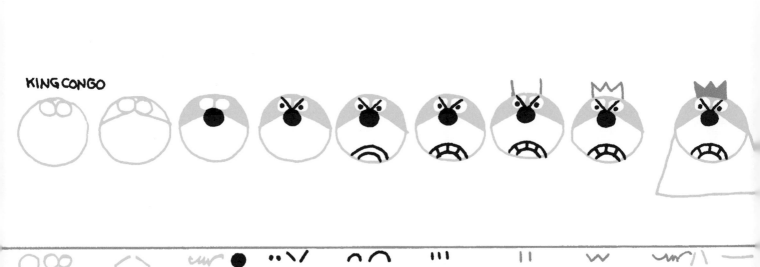

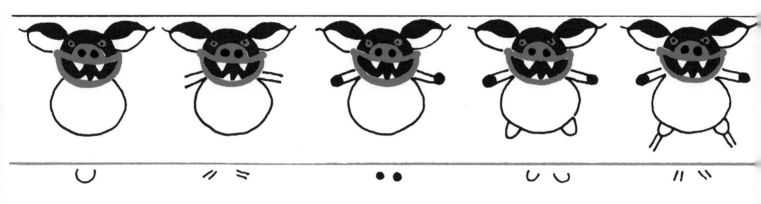

VAMPIRE

ALSO

21

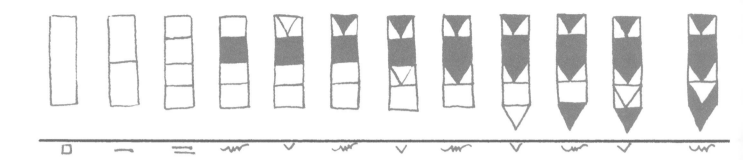

MR. HYDE

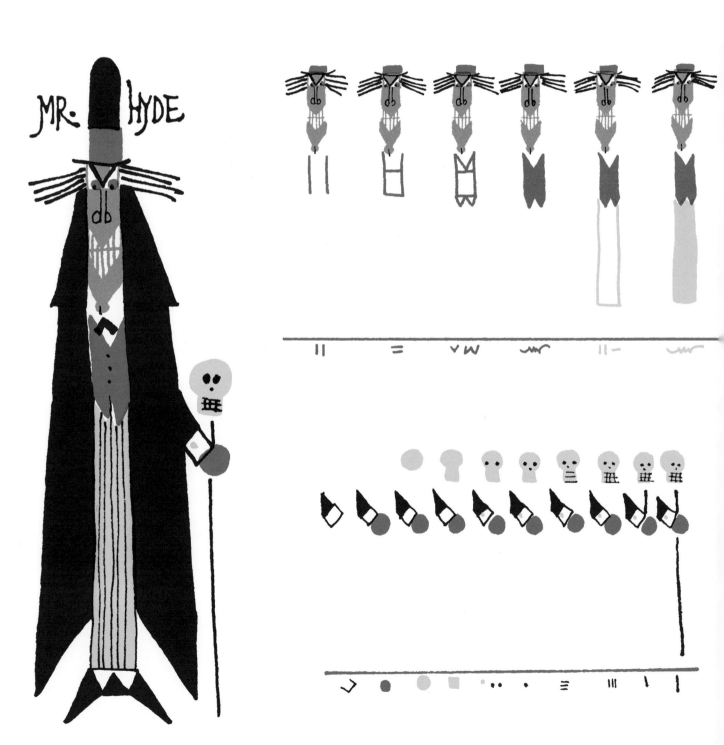

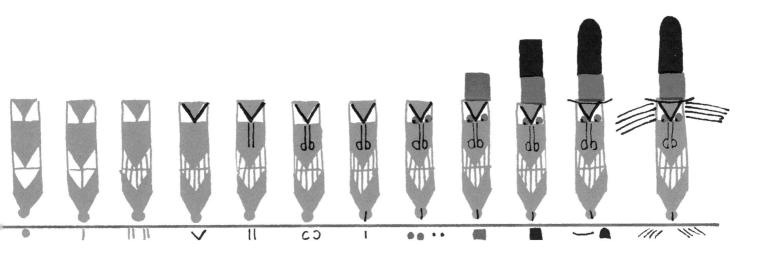

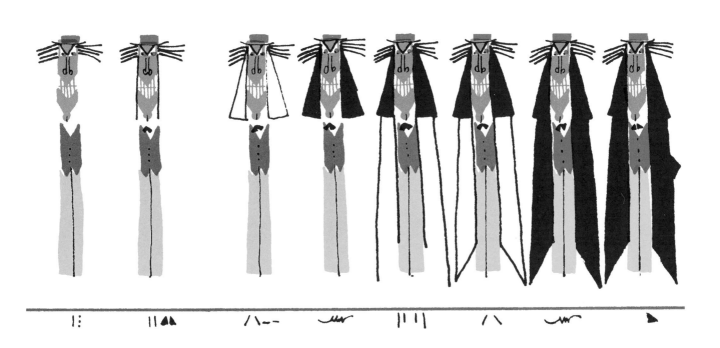

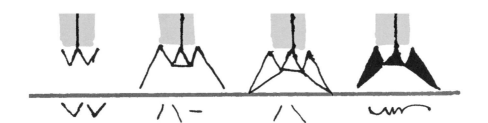

KING CONGO

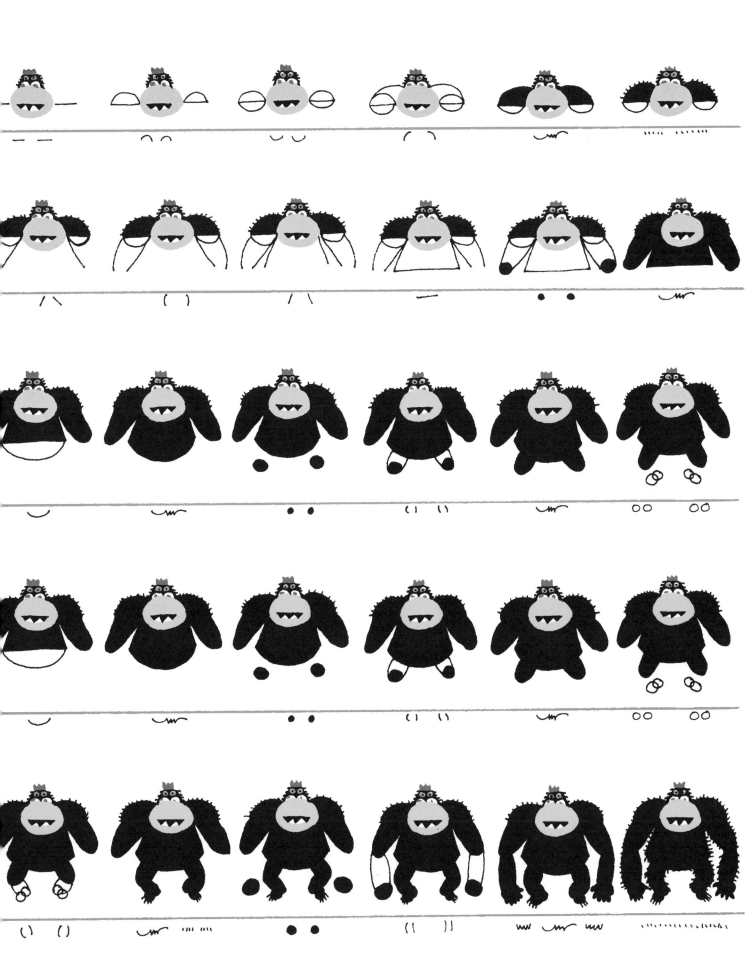

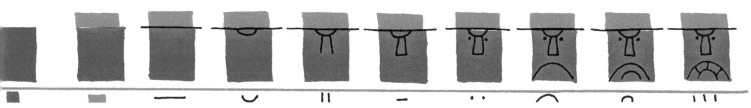

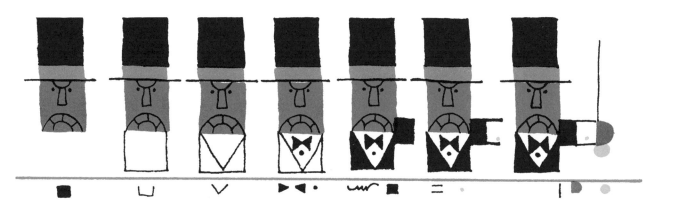

MR. HYDE

NAPOLEON
BONYPARTS

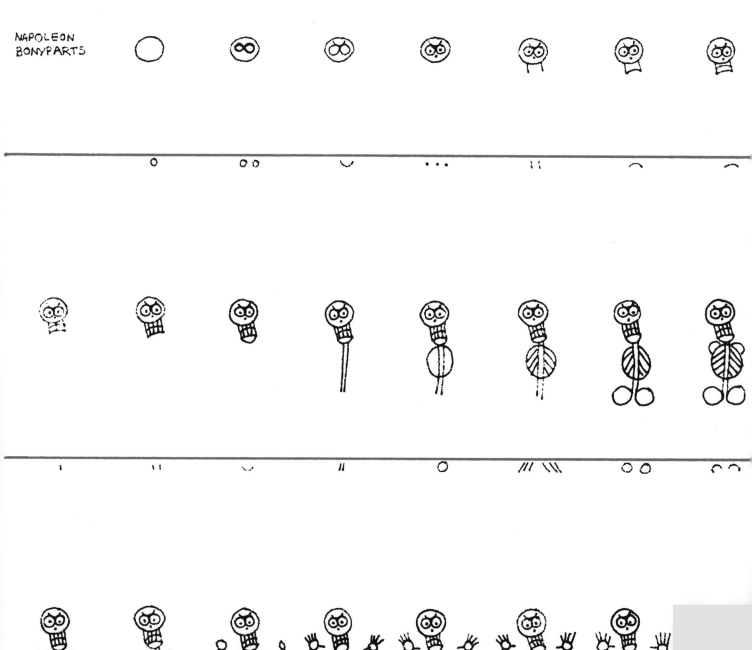

ALSO

30

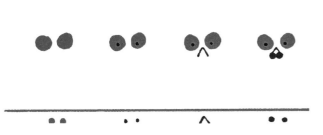

NAPOLEON BONYPARTS

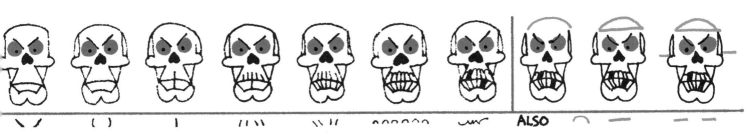

ALSO

N

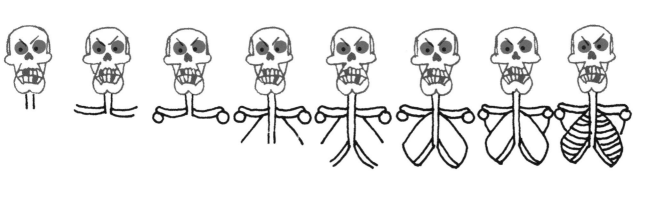

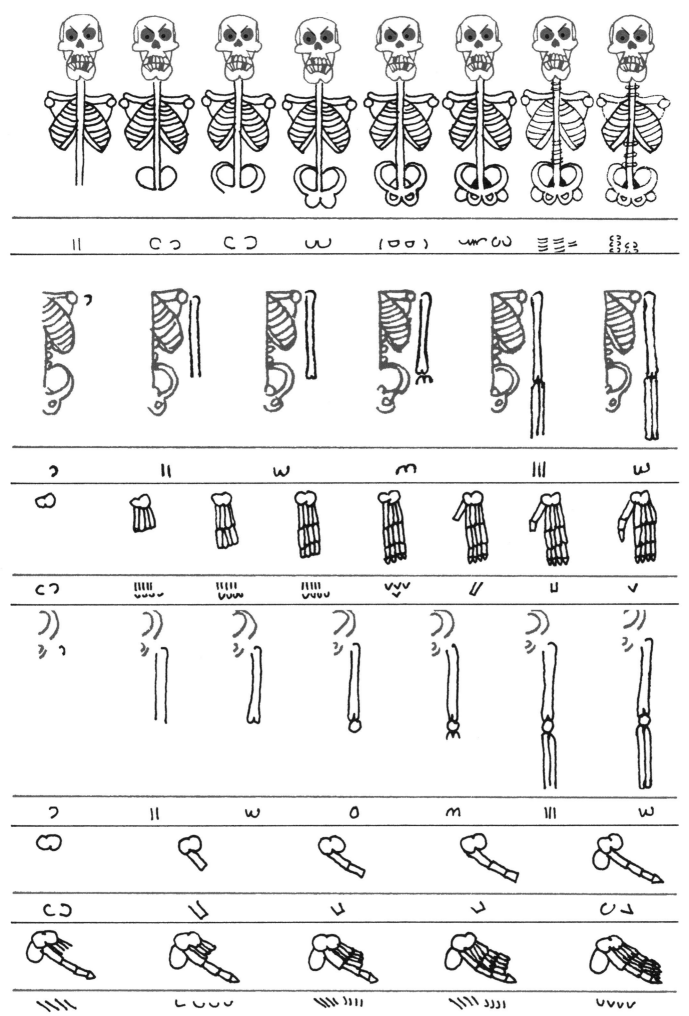

HALLOWEEN SILHOUETTES

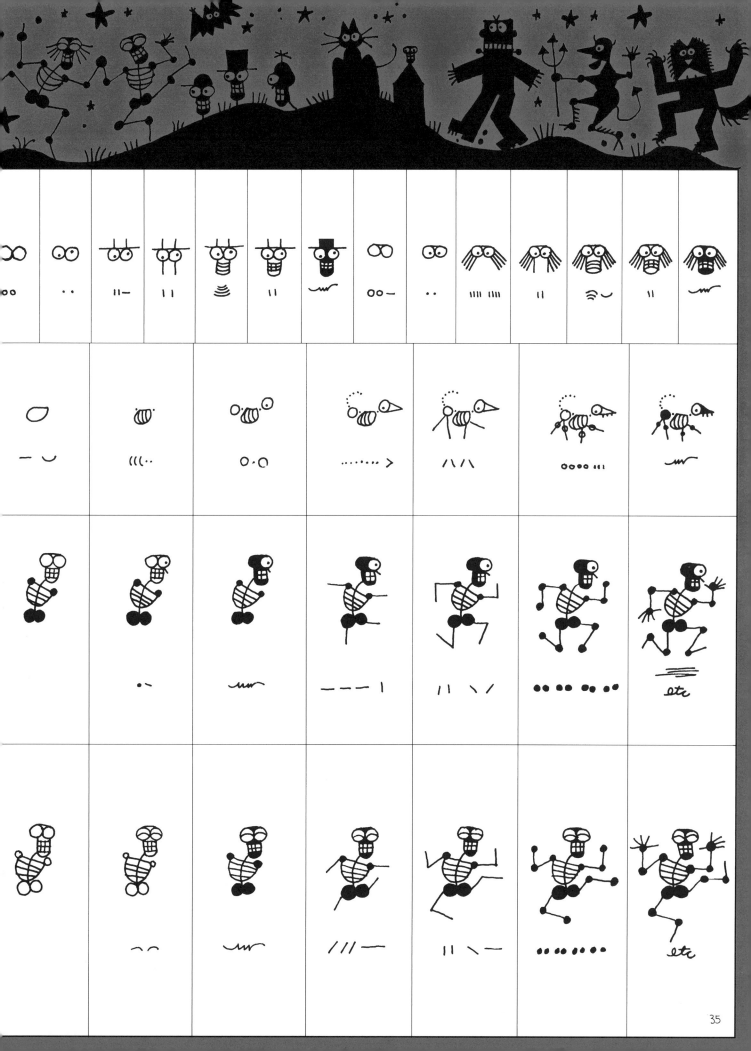

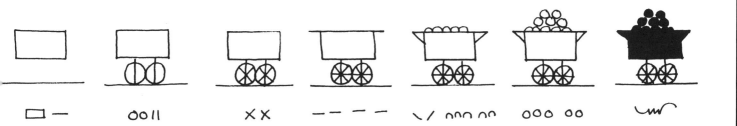

□ —   OO I I   X X   — — — —   \ / ∩∩∩ ∩∩   OOO OO   ∿

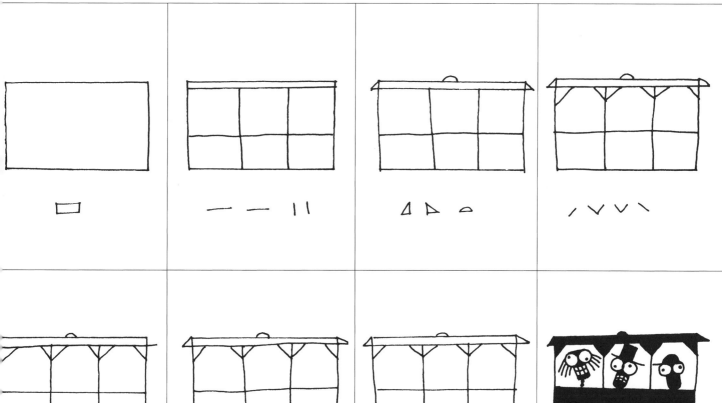

□   — — — I I   △ △ ◠   / \ ∨ ∨ \

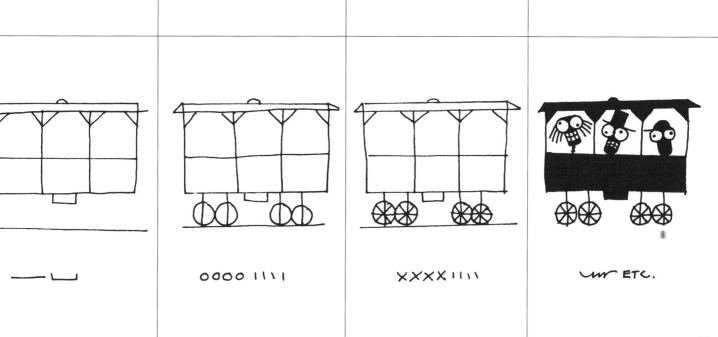

— ⊔   OOOO I I I I   XXXX I I I I   ∿ ETC.

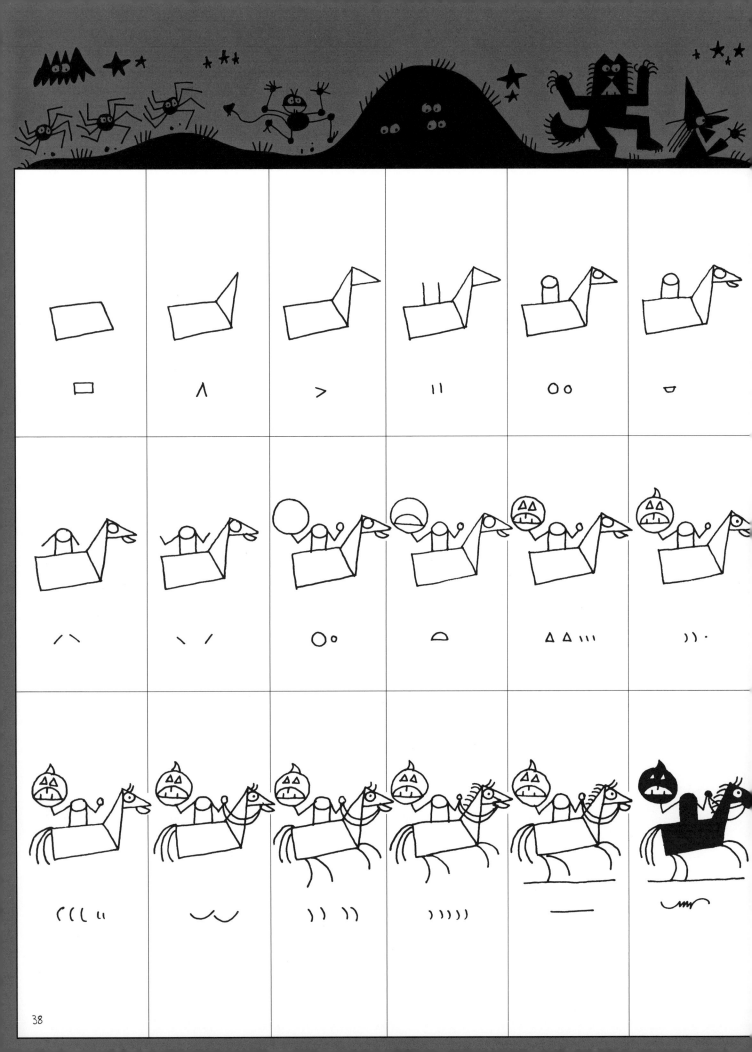

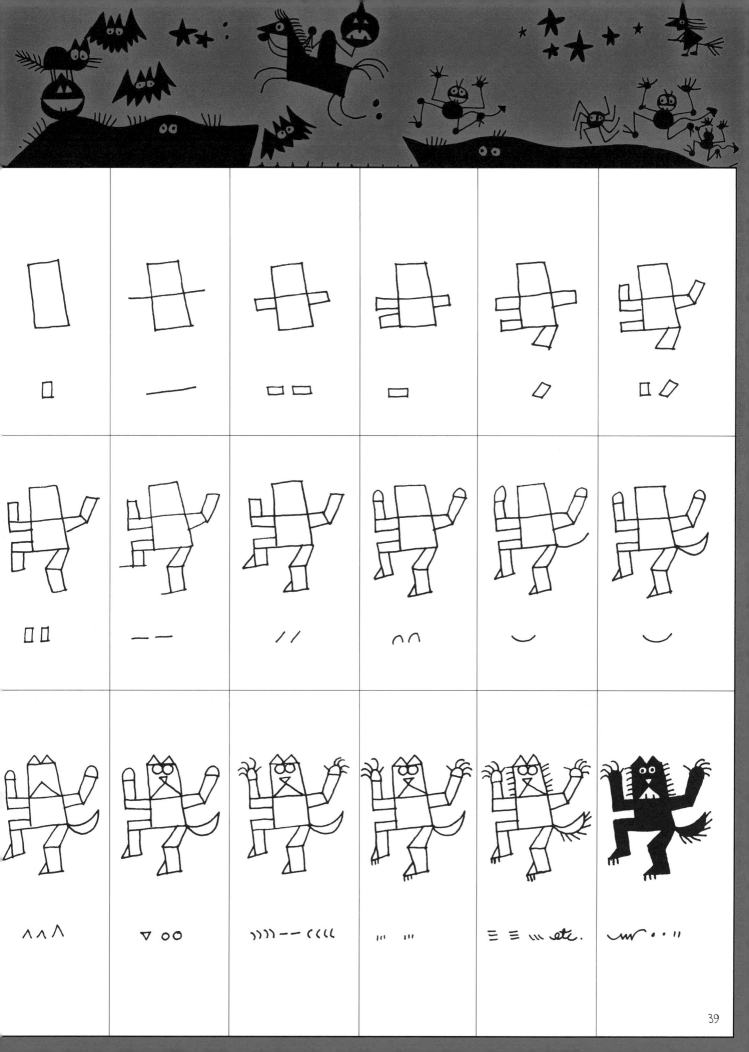

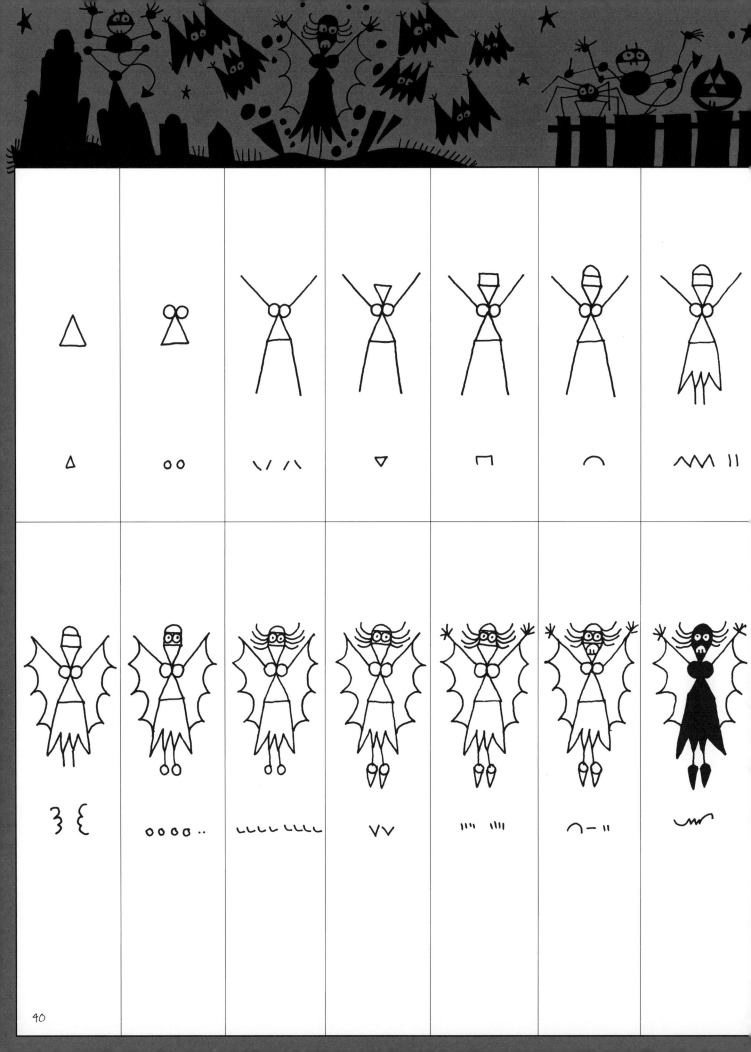

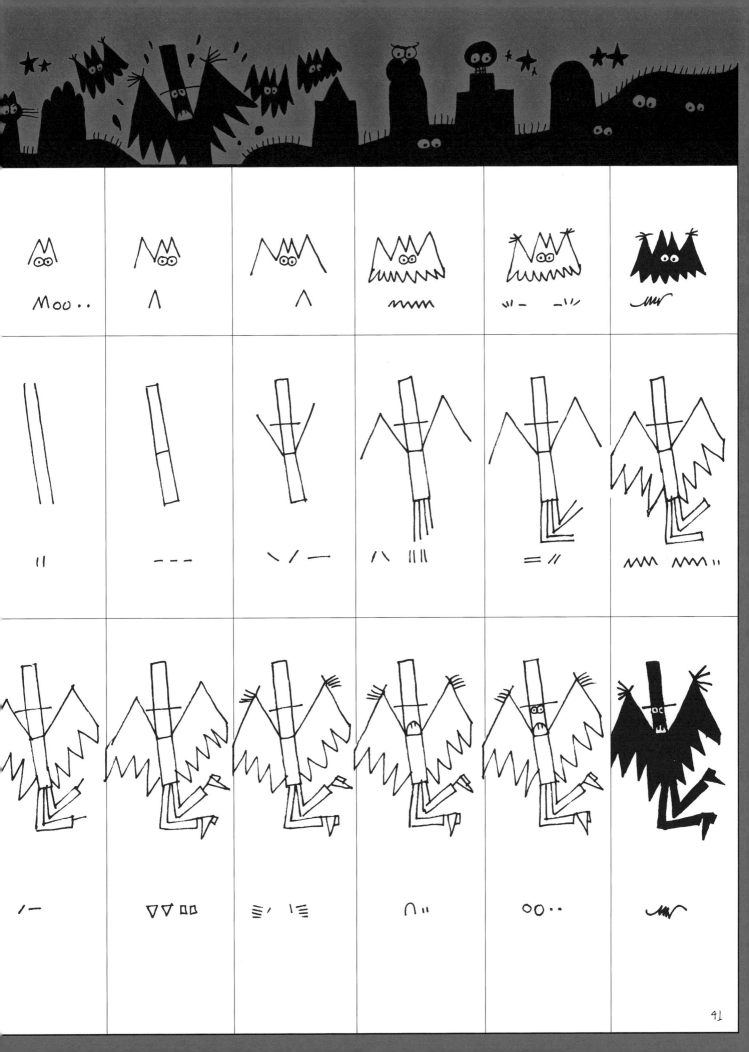

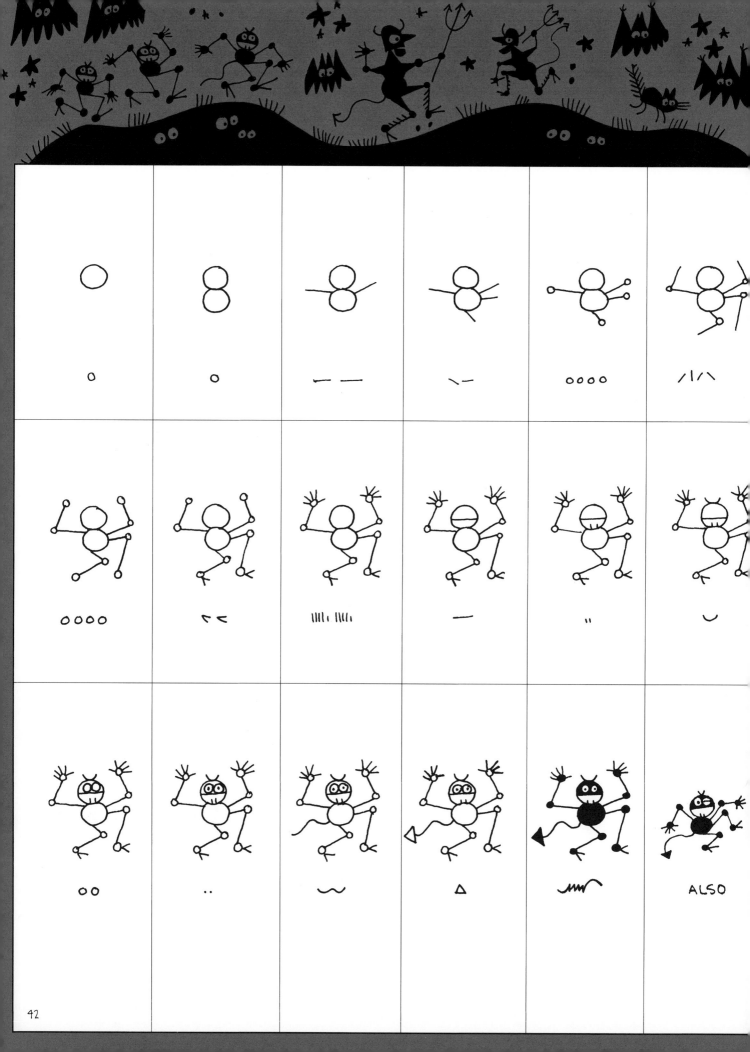

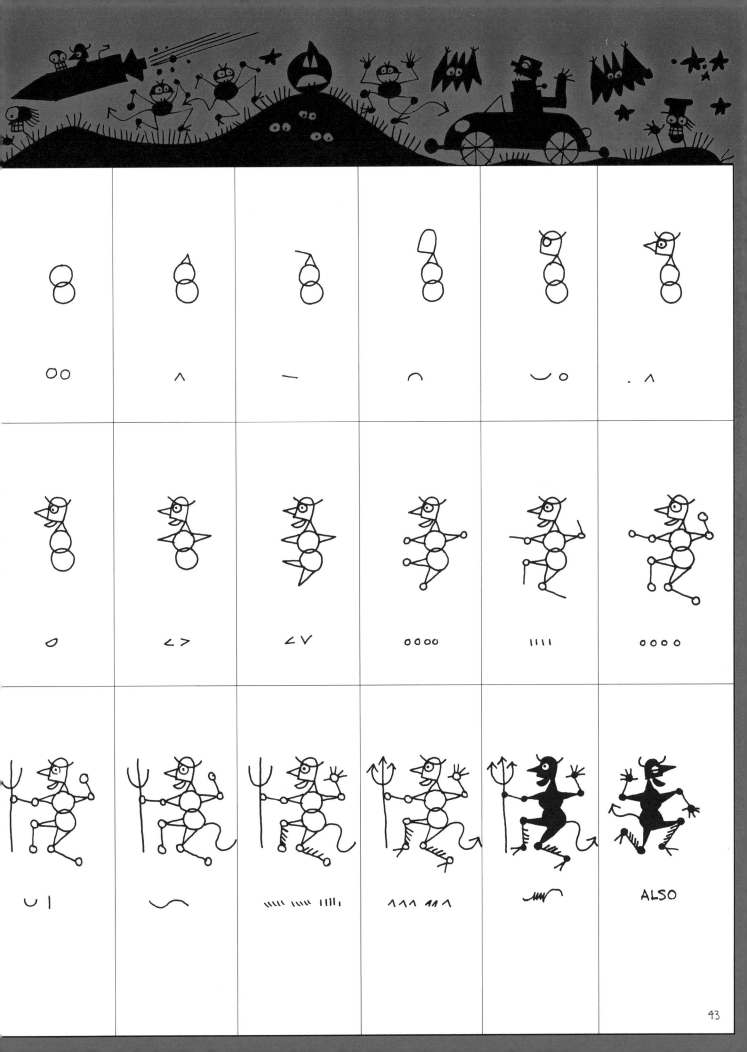

ALSO

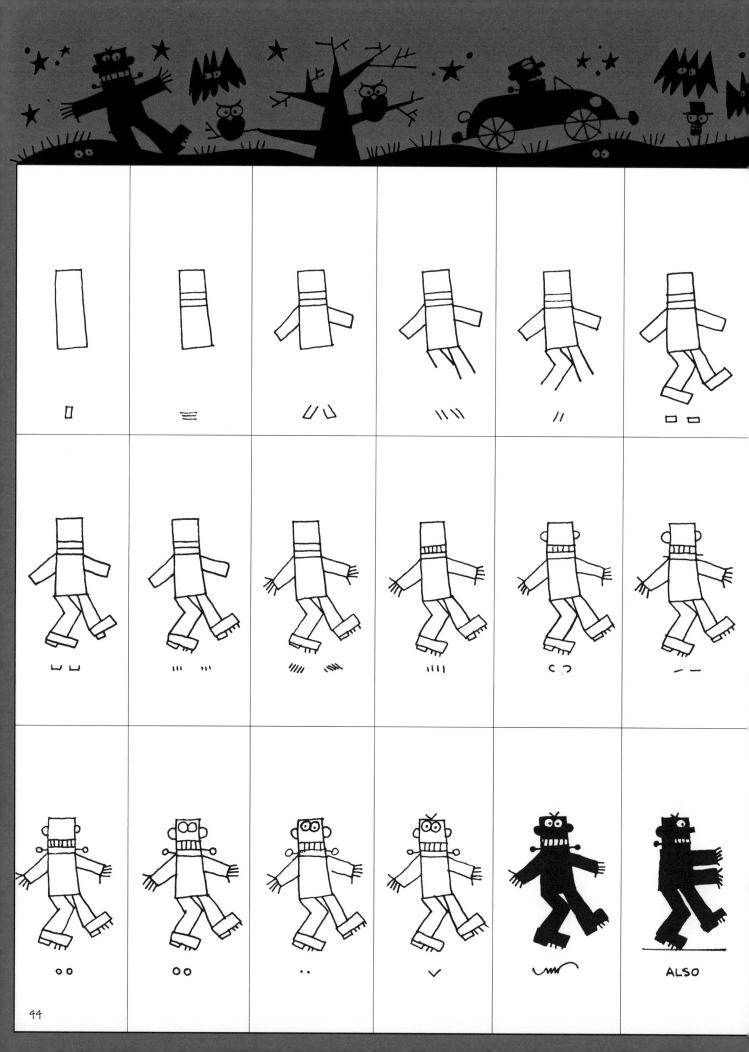

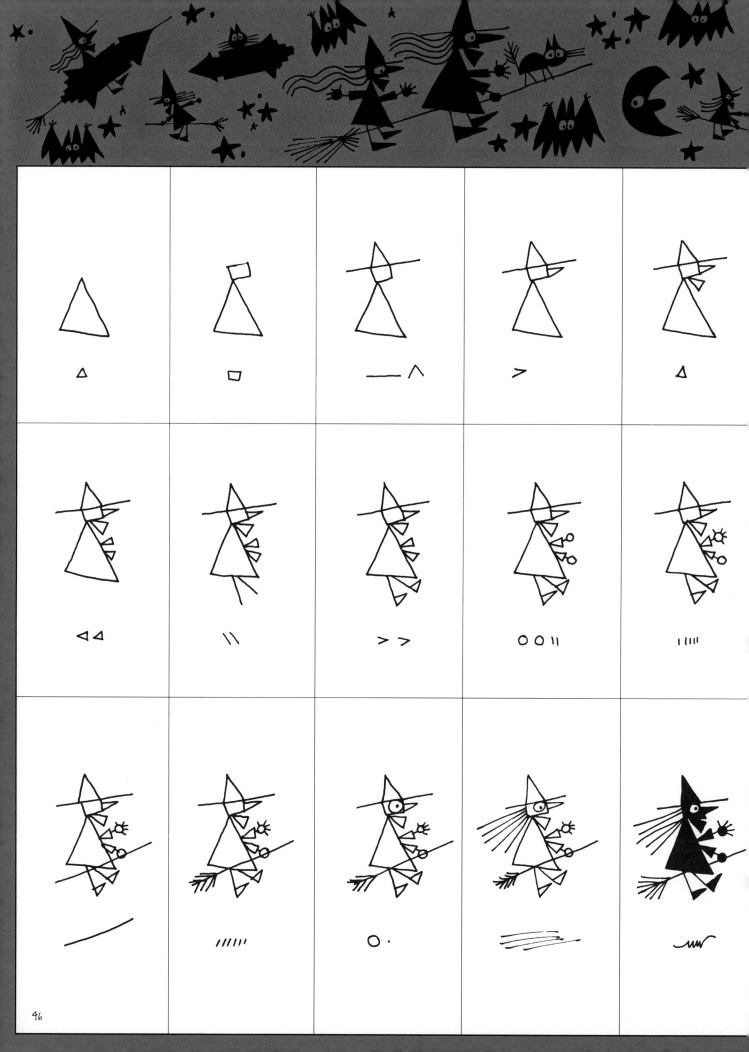

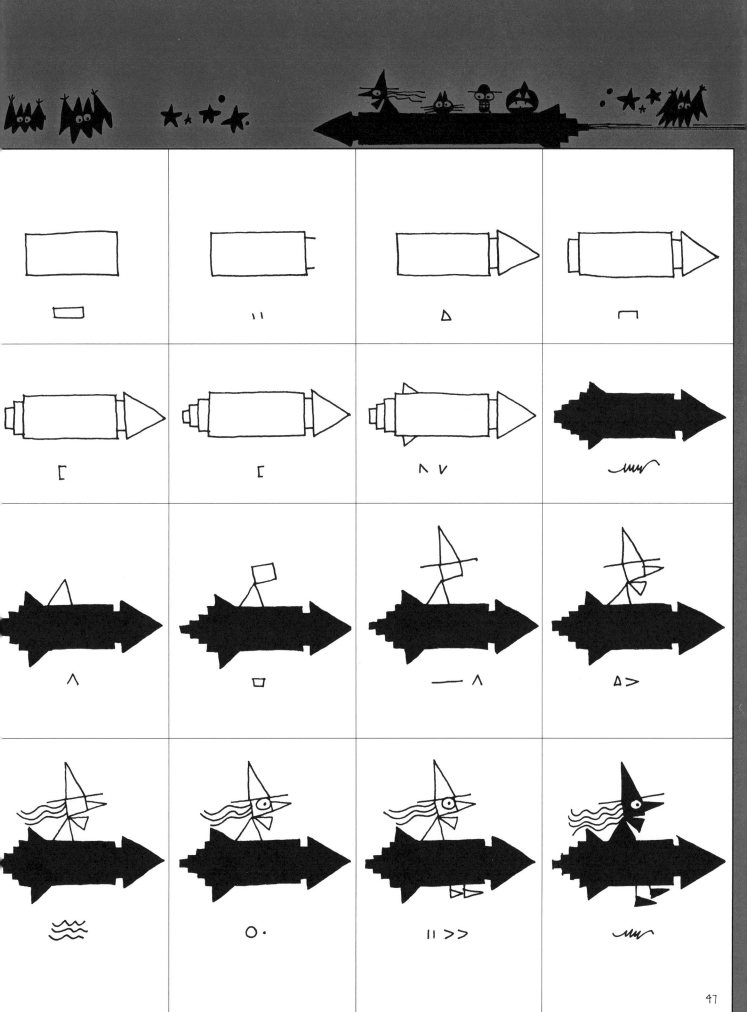

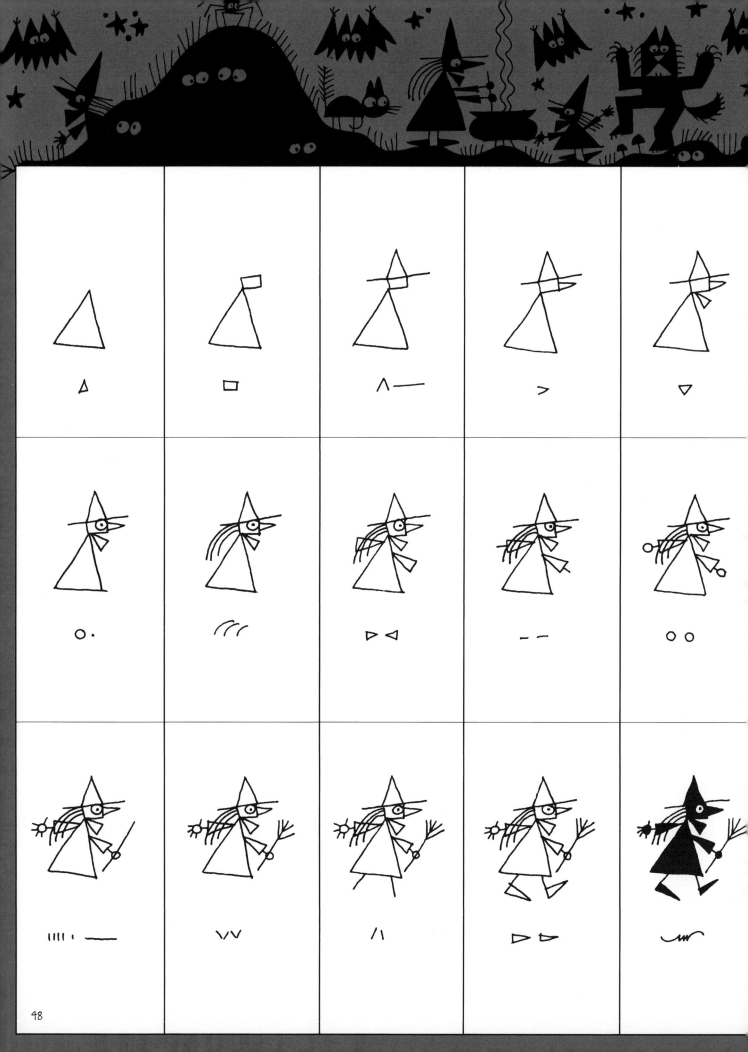

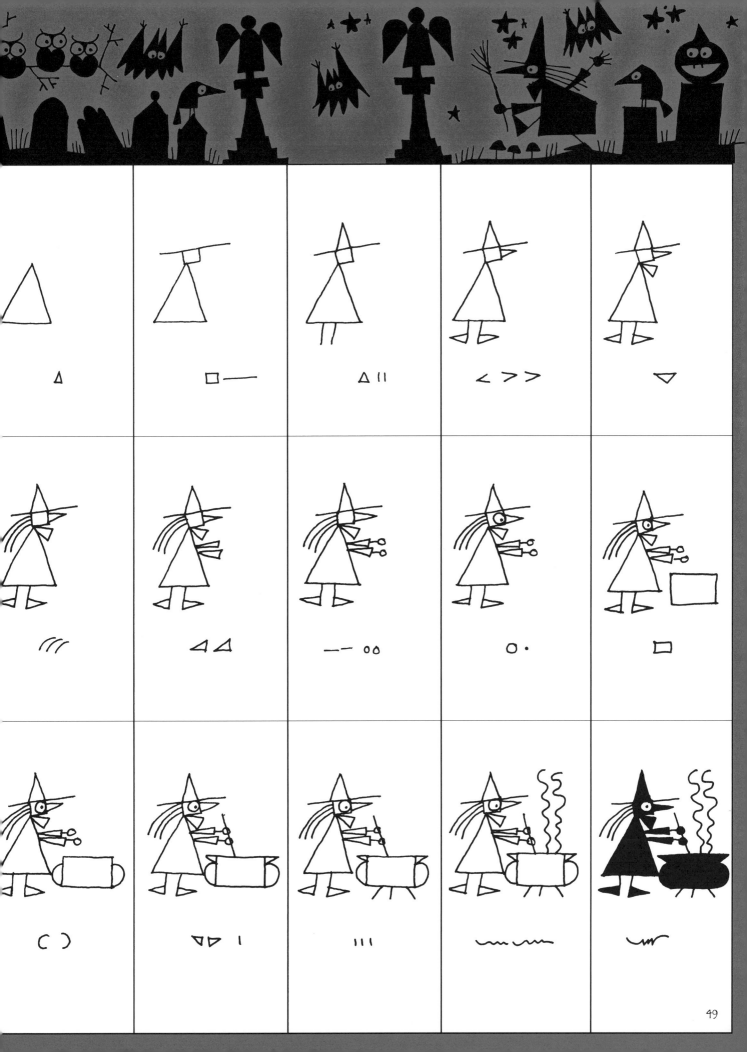

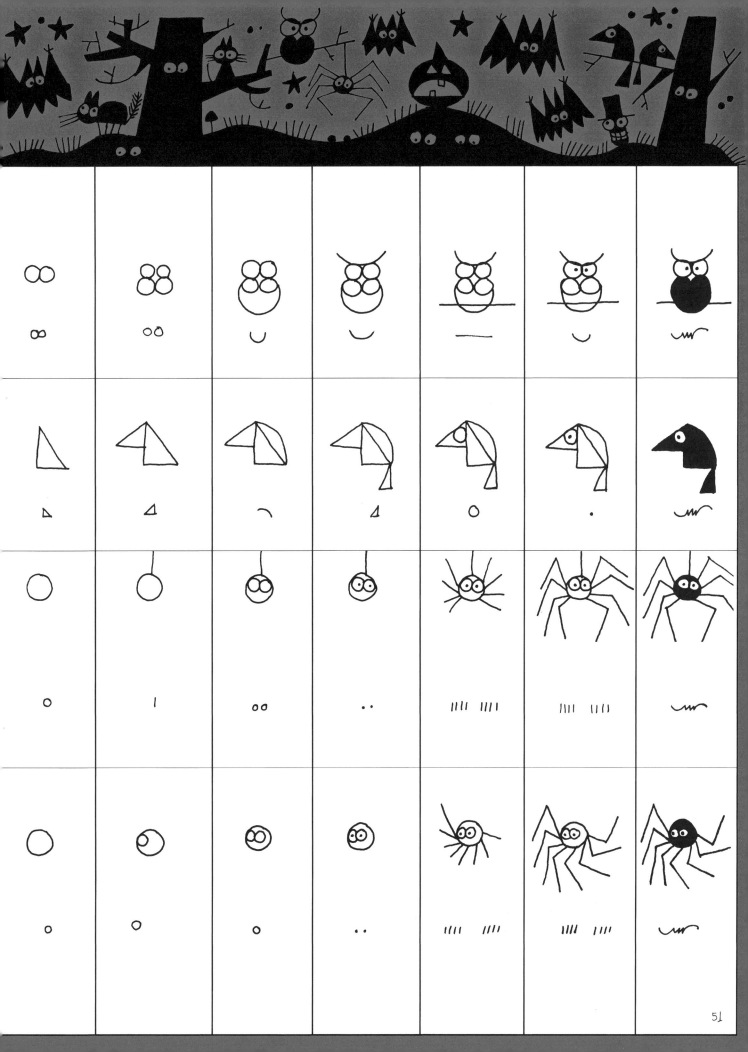

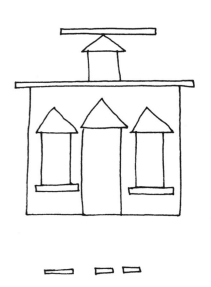

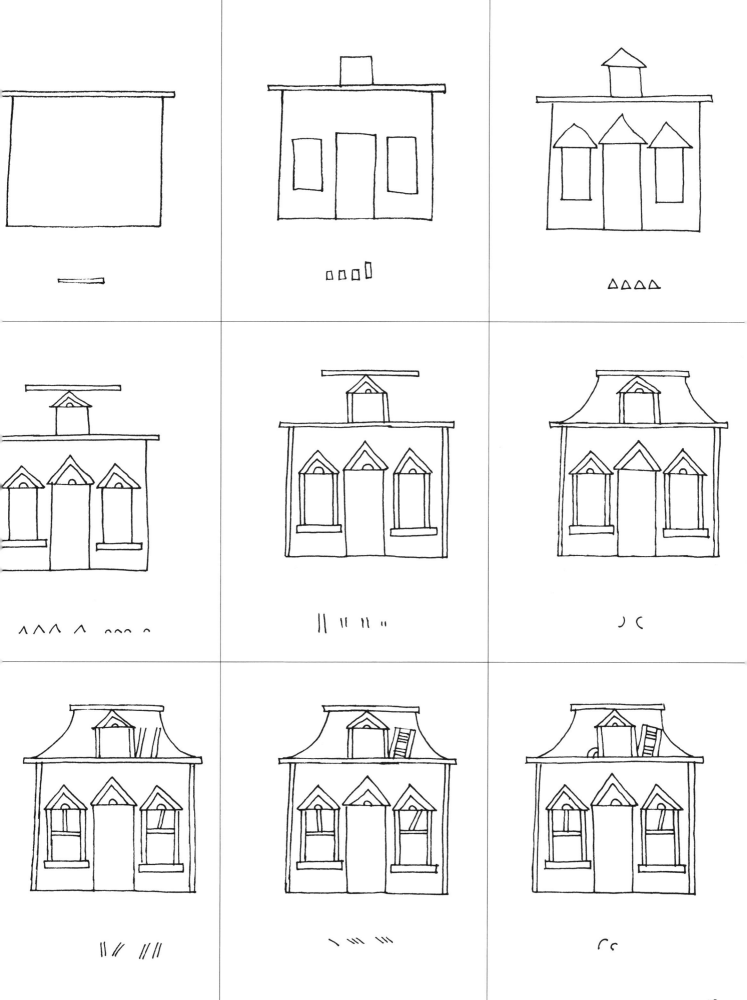

V U etc.

ETC.

etc.

ALSO

ALSO

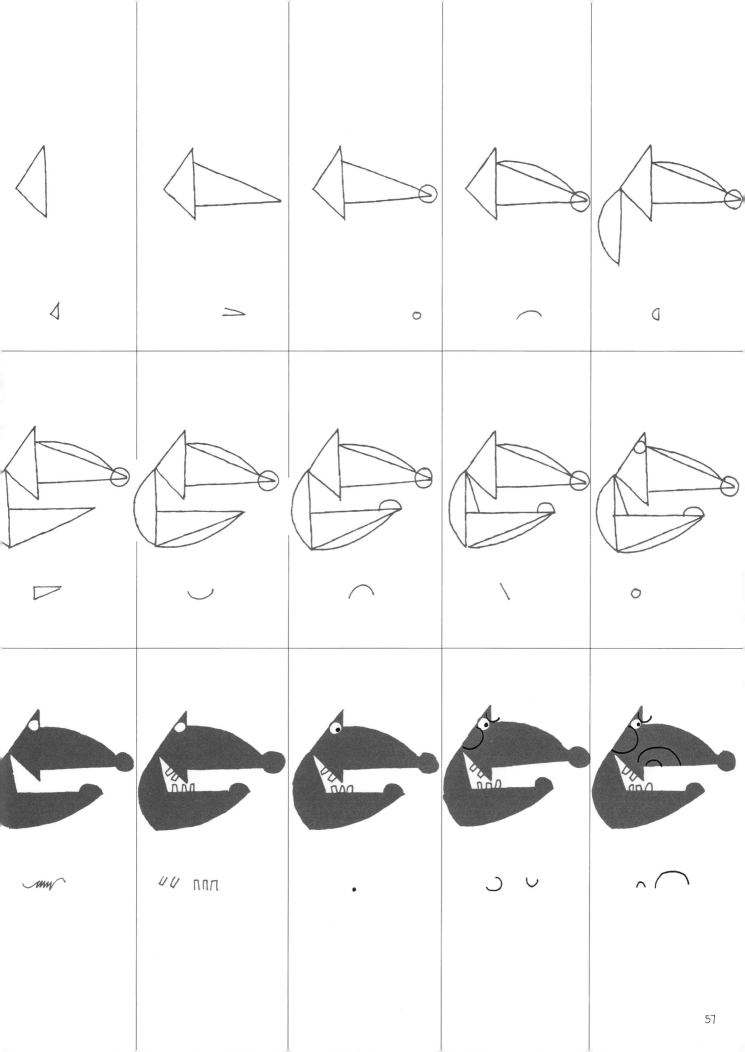

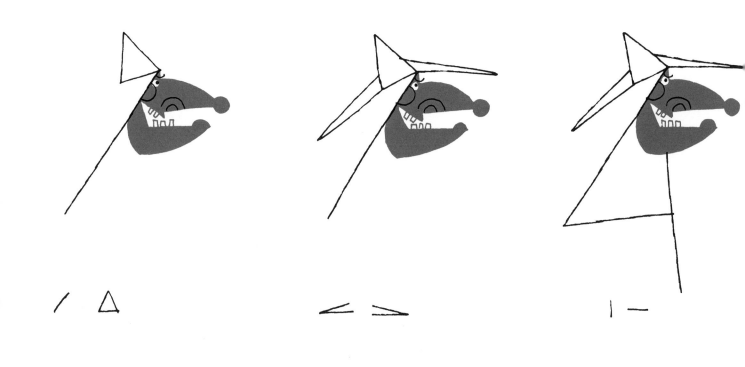

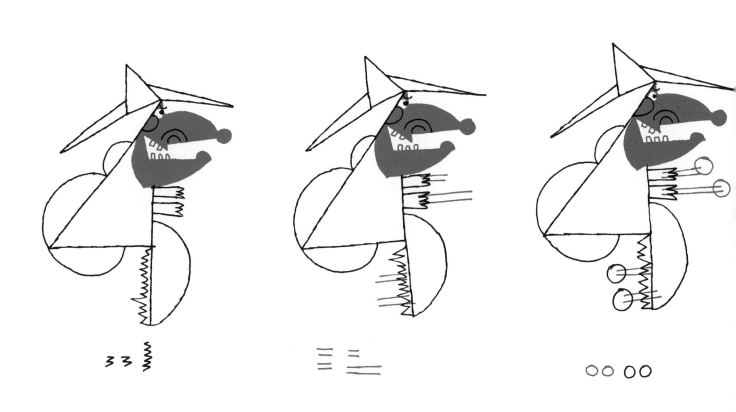

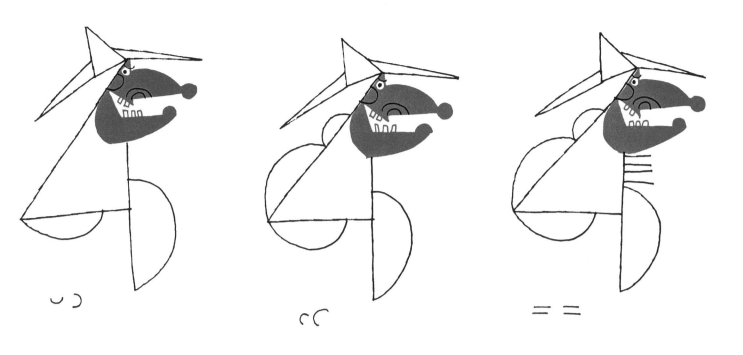

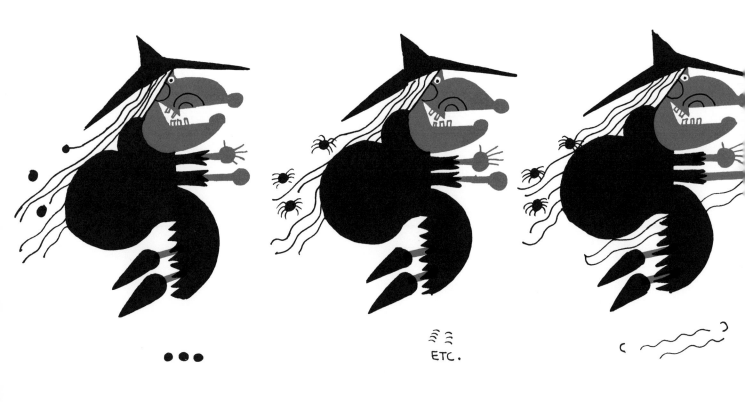

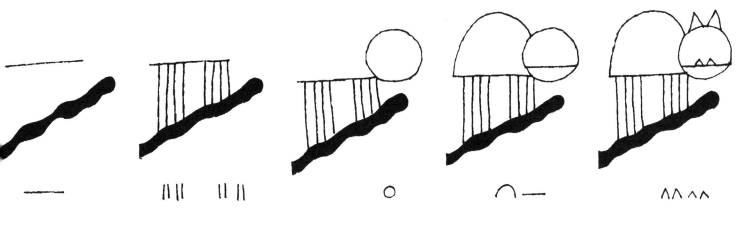

USE THIS SPACE TO DRAW YOUR OWN MONSTERS!

For more creepy-crawly monsters to draw, look for:

Swamp Creature
in *Ed Emberley's Big Purple*
Drawing Book

Greengrin, Mr. Hyde, Frank,
Dracula, and Dracula's Car
in *Ed Emberley's Big Green*
Drawing Book